*O*ut

of the Rain

conversations

with   spaces

between

leaves

Out of the Rain,
conversations with spaces between leaves
by Stephen P. Redic
All Rights Reserved.

Photo collages by www.PamelaBeckerCreations.com
Book Design by Pamela Becker
Book Edited by Blue Moon
www.SedonaBlueMoon.com

Published 2008
ISBN 978-0-9817830-8-6

POETRY

BY

STEPHEN P. REDIC

Introduction…

I learn to write, and then the writing takes over. As a child, my mother read to me. She read classics like Black Beauty and Treasure Island. She read the Bible. Then she told me to read anything and everything -setting me free. This love of literature was the seed that became the desire to write. I write and I imagine and I write some more. Then I rewrite. The truth is and it has its own sound and rhythm.

I started to write in high school. It became a passion as I matured- an addiction, which I made no effort to cure. I am infected with the "storyteller" gene. Like any good performer, a writer must entertain and tell a story- not necessarily in that order. Writing, whether in prose or poetry, tells a story. This story is about turning life into poetry.

Writing in sudden bursts, and then rewriting several weeks later, has become a ritual. It allows a detachment from the moment, and a measure of how well the writing brings back the feeling or "tells" the story. Sometimes picking the right word, like so many flowers of a bouquet, or so many sounds of the human voice, is as simple as saying less.

"Let the rose say everything about its' color."

In many ways, I consider myself to be a very lucky man. At the age of 45, I was reunited with my birth parents and family. Some people might think that would have given a person a lot to write about. It did exactly the opposite. Almost a year passed and I had no inspiration or desire to write. Then it happened. I was at a construction site watching the goings on, and with pencil and paper began to write down my observations. Like an alcoholic taking a drink, I couldn't stop.

When I speak of love, it's because I've been blessed. Several times in my life, I have loved and been loved back. There is no greater wealth that a person can have. The poem "Hunter's Moon" speaks of a love between the sun and moon, with "Mother Earth" standing guard against the passion. In the poem, "Moment", I talk of love that spans the ages and while unique in each incarnation is also the same in its potential. "Without" was written as wedding vows to my wife, Pat, who has encouraged and supported me in all my endeavors. "Honor" speaks of a love that cannot be- yet exists as hope until the end. The two poems, "Flint" and "Lighthouse", were written as examples of love in absence. Most recent, the poem, "Of Love" is the sum of experience looking back at the equation and recognizing the balance.

This book is the result of a challenge. My friends challenged me, as all good friends should, to write something that spoke the truth about how I really felt. Good writing should ask the questions that everyone is thinking- but no one dares to speak. It is by questioning that we learn; it is by doing that we teach. It is by telling the "story" that we pass it forward in hopes that we will never forget reasons or the consequences of our actions. "I believe," may be the two most powerful words in any language. That one phrase allows, each-and-every-person, to rise up and make their selves better today than they were yesterday. More importantly, when one takes the "leap of faith" to believe in someone else, you give the greatest gift of all.

I took this "leap" with my eyes wide open, knowing that some would like this collection and others wouldn't. For those that do, I hope you're smiling, because that was my purpose, my promise, my belief. For those that don't- go read something else, life's too short for bad stories!

Dream/prayer

May your dreams have many paths,
That lead you to a friend.
May your days be filled with colors,
And happy without end.
May your heart be filled with love
Enough for all to share,
May all you wishes become real,
And all your hopes be fair.
May your hands be found
In all good deeds,
May you find the time
to plant a seed.
May those that need you most
Be always in your reach,
May those that need you least
Be the ones you teach.
Let all these things
Be yours
To share with those you touch,
While you remember well these words,
"You never can, love too much."

The Wolf

Cry not for the wolf,
He dreams of you,
Under the fangs
Of a crescent moon.

Short,
Panting,
Gasps/
Echo
On hollow
howling
Wind.
Shadows
Cling close
Like
Original sin.

Cry not for the wolf,
He dreams of you,
Painting the dawn
With crimson hues.

Morning star,
Cyclops's eye,
Sunlight melts
Night/black sky.
Teapots whistle,
Bands march on,
Cry not, "The wolf!"
The night is gone.

Afternoon Shadows

Shimmer as velvet highlights
Slide into dusk
Of back country road.
Harlot winter
Dances through pine cone
To birch branch,
Offering her cold
For your fire,
Her naked charms
For your church,
Your time
for her quiet questions
Suggestions
Of desire.
She snaps
Her demands,
Like fingers
In a jazz bar,
Moving with no mind,
Searching for something
with nothing to find.
She settles for cigarettes,
Slowly smoldering
Into
Grey/white
Ash.

ove at Mcdonalds

Like Mcdonalds?
Oh love is not!
Although…….
Sometimes it's quick,
And sometimes it's hot!

You can eat it in,
You can eat it out,
You can get it in a drive thru-
But you'll have to shout!

Sometimes it's messy and
Gets on your shirt,
And sometimes you have it
Right out in the dirt.

Oh, Love at Mcdonalds-
Oh, What a deal!
Love at Mcdonalds-
The real happy meal.

alloon

I dream that dream,
Of my balloon.
The one that says,
"Get well soon."

I heal,
And set it free,
And just like me
It drifts past trees,
Tangling branch with wind,
Until it leaves my sight,
Filling itself
With evening sky blues.

I dream those dreams,
Those dreams of you,
That so real seams,
That I am fooled.
Where there is no need
For war and greed,
Where peace becomes
The planted seed.
They take my breath away,
Make my feet move
My body sways,
Between heartbeats,
like thunder
Before rain,
Explodes on city streets.
I dream that dream.

No More

No More!
Used, abused,
No more!!
Battered, bruised,
No more!
Helpless, confused.

Eye to eye,
Heart to hate,
Fists of anger,
A loving mate?

No more lies,
No more ties,
Just no more
Sad goodbyes.
Head held high
Filled with pride,
No more bruises
I have to hide.

Enough is enough-
When I'm down on the floor!
Enough is too much!
Enough/
No more.

lowns

If you see the fire,
Do you smell the smoke?
If the clown falls down,
Do you get the joke?

Can you be happy
With milk fed veal,
While children starve
for lack of a meal?

The water we drink
As the oil we spill,
Soon won't even
a thimble fill.

If all the rain forests
Become extinct,
Will that make mankind
more distinct?

A badger might its foot to escape,
But shooting students
Is government rape.

When babies in the carriages,
Are carrying guns,
And the ozone surrenders
Your skin to the sun,
Politics won't matter
And money won't buy,
If questions aren't asked,
Answers will lie.

If you see the fire,
Is it just smoke?
When the clown falls down,
Is it a joke?

February

We arrive,
Singles,
And pairs,
Before the best seats fill.

We touch
Their hands,
Waiting for the truth,
To grip our fingers.

We watch,
Half expecting them to wake,
As though startled from their sleep
By all this attention.

The young are restless,
And want to play.
The old are tired,
Counting their time in minutes,
And by the day,
Until it is their chance to dream.

Only the priest is late,
But it's not his funeral.

Honor

Who knows the heart,
That feels the pain,
That drives the man
To go insane?

Who chooses the dance
On fields of battle,
Where cannons roar
And machine guns rattle?

For honor and Queen,
He loves to death.
Secrets pass
With parting breath.

What common man
Should be her king?
What cruel fate
Would conceive this thing?

To love that which
Cannot love back,
To desire all,
Yet all to lack.

lected

Buick
Park Avenue wrapped,
Business white shirt,
Early work-tee time three,
Cuts traffic,
Leaving no tracks
On rough concrete.

Elections of government,
Spending more than
Their/our fair share,
Passing pretense
That they care.
Keeping power in
Power's hand,
Reaping profit
Raping land.

Year in/year out
Politicians jump/shout,
"Give me a chance!"
Kick the other bum out!

All bought and sold
On auction block,
Cattle to the slaughter,
executions electric shock,
Drowning in the water,
Hold your breath,
Don't inhale,
Save the world!
Save a whale!

oops

The sun:
Drips sweat
On melting players.
Each drop
An echo of the heartbeats
That pound on the court.

The court:
Carved white lines,
Coal black tar,
A lane,
A key, a baseline
Boundary.
A stage for split-second
One act plays,
Called the "shot.'

The shot:
Momentary miracle,
Fluid touch
-reach for the sky,
"I'll never die!"
Pulling a piece of time
From bottom of hoop-
Inevitable arc:
Replaced by swish of net
Caressing orange colored ball.

The ball,
The reason
We all love this game,
This game called hoops.

unger

I

Hunger
For my father's blows and beatings…
That I may know his touch.

I

Long to hear his voice
Cursing my name…
That I may be acknowledged.

I

smell his alcoholic habit,
And know ….
My inheritance is ordained.

I

Think as mad or insane,
Or perhaps just crazy,
As happens to those
in solitary cells,
Where bars and walls
Are gray and hazy.
Where any past will do
To pass the time
And pay your dues
Where there is nothing to forget
And less to remember,
And I am left
Alone
To choose.

I

Stand
Unforgiving
For that
which I have not done,
I am the prodigal
First born seventh son.

othing

It wasn't much,
Not any more,
A look,
A touch,
A nearby distant shore.
Night time hum,
Snoring bum,
Keeping park bench paint
And newsprint page
Warm and wet,
Like July storm.
Through haze,
Across the maze
Of silent sentinel trees,
Shadows and shades
Of life on the
Fringe of light,
Rent unpaid
At the moment of truth,
Empties the clip
Into the dark,
Scares pigeons, pimps,
And hookers
Out
Of the park
As bullets race
To find the fights.
Headlights move past
The flash of cash.
It's nothing,
At least,
not now.

ullaby

Sing me a lullaby,
In the slow sweet rhythms
Of the sea.
Let my heart rest,
On fingers of swaying evergreens,
Tickled by shy young winds.

Hold me in your arms,
As mountains cradle valleys
As we slumber with the sly grins of youth.
In the peace of our love
And cool shadows of our souls,
Sing me a lullaby
Softly and slow.

lint

In the shadows
Of my soul,
I walk alone.
I will fear
No darkness,
For you
are my light.
I rest
as your touch
Excites me,
Electric race
Without finish.
I die in flames,
Without regret,
Reborn in rhythms
Of your love,
Dancing in quiet night.
Across desert sands,
I thirst for your lips,
Whispers to cool
My fever,
Gentle breezes,
of twilight air.
My dreams consume me.
I am tinder
to your flint.

I wake.

Hunter's Moon

Haunted Hunter's Moon,
hangs low in mornings' eye,
Escapes the dream,
That is the night.
Daring all to fly.

Shed your garments
of golden/red rust,
Let fall
Upon the autumn floor.
Smile your smile
of innocence,
Virgin bride
at bedroom door.

To rule as Queen
Of sleepless night,
Or stand a moment…
In lover's sight.
To feel the heat
Of passions' kiss…
Or hide forever
In twilight's mist.

To feel the pain
Of love once lost,
To know the price,
But not the cost,
Sunlight sparkles
On moonlight's' frost.

Secret Wish

Corner
Window stares
Into dimly dense
Backyard brush.
Sudden shifting movement,
And He is there.
We are both early risers.

Motionless, Breathless,
He seeks
To again become one of the trees,
Little birch, tall pine, old oak.

He will not run,
I would not.
We are both warriors,
We have both fought.

Geese announce their departure,
Mornings air filled with honking chorus.
Air, so softly damp
With anticipatory rain,
Holding its heartbeat
With love for the sun.

Our eyes lock/stare straight
While trying to see
Behind the corners of our vision,
Trying to glance
Beyond the horizon of surprise.

Then… He is gone.
Mists turn their back
On care filled land,
Carrying freedom to the sky,
Slowly waving goodbye.
Silently climbing into clouds.
Secretly wishing.

ircle

In a circle
Sit the seekers,
Silent silhouettes
of time collapsed.
In the center,
sit's the one,
Seeking wisdom
of the past.

Slowly slithers the solemn chant,
Eyes speak more than words can say,
Vision has a different slant.
Motions swift
Voice staccato,
Crystals from
Some secret grotto.
Seize thought, splash time,
Ask no question,
Commit no crime.

Spinning sparks
Dance dervish swirls,
Into circle and out again.
Seekers scream in holy chorus,
Into circle and out again.
Floating, soaring, sweeping, weeping
Into circle and out again.

Silent seekers
Watch dancing flames
As burning embers
Erase the names.
Into circle and out again,
Only the night and moon remain.

*I*nside/out

Winter's death
Becomes
First breath,
Blossom's fragrance,
Youthful innocence,
Dripping
Together
From naked limb,
Surrenders life to life,
Fortune to fate or
Foe,
Love for all
That do not know.
I whisper
Silence to your silence.
I wait.
Time waits longer.
I hold you.
You are not here.
I dream.

Of Love

It is the light
That feeds the heart,
A fuel that burns
With single spark,
The shiver
Of a warm welcome touch,
The coldness
Of being alone-
Too often, too much.
The anticipation
Of a chance to meet,
The assassin's blade
Dipped in promises
With secrets to keep.
It is the hunger
Of newborn day,
Devouring night,
Until morning decides to stay.
It plays the wind
With harmonic chime,
Marking moments
With vibrations of time.
It is all, that it is not,
Then something even more.
It is
The puzzle, the key,
The open door.

ickett's Charge

Hot as hell,
Damn Yankee summer.
Ain't no breeze,
'ceptin' the drummer,
Beatin' time… beatin' time…
Cheatin' time along.

Long gray lines begin to walk,
A final march, towards a silent grove.
Beatin' time, beatin' time,
Cheat time along.

Form and fire-
Black smoke/coats throat-
Cannons roar demanding lunch,
Clark brothers
Die in a bunch.
Beat time, Beat time,
Step quick, pray hard!
Cheat time-charge!

Almost there.
Hope to make it,
If I don't-
Named pinned on coat.
Beat time/beat.

Yankee cannon in my sights,
Touch match/fire true
Smokey gray/blue
Uniforms
Fall to earth/no sound,
Bleeding hope on holy ground.

Beat time… Beat time
Cheat.
Ain't no breeze/ 'ceptin' the drummer.

Old Man

Just an old man,
Doesn't know
Pine from oak or fir,
Staring at the trees…

Look at him!
Cupping his hand
To catch the wind,
His senses have left
For a different land…

Come in old man!
Before you catch cold,
Or death finds you outside
After dark…

My trees they talk to me
Slow ageless whispers,
Not of themselves,
But of the space between leaves,
I listen as a child.

My winds,
They carry spirits,
Smoke adrift the clouds
Bearing songs
Of the lonely heart,
Knowing all that is
Must soon part.

My setting sun,
Let me watch,
And feel the warmth
Seducing fragrance from
Fresh mown hay,
Let me be, as I am,
The end of another day.

Parade

Watch the people,
Watching people.
Stranger eye
That eyes the strangers.
Without reflection,
Without affection,
Voiceless murmur,
Without inflection.
Parading by
Step
By step,
Until the final monkey,
Banging brass cymbals
To his own beat,
Sideways slide,
Two left feet.

ierce

I pierce
To feel the pain,
To hunger,
So deep,
As others do,
To feel the difference,
Not in my blue/green
Red streaked hair,
But in nails/black
Like lips the color of death,
Waiting in lines,
Tattooed and tattered
Like maps to nowhere,
Folded and wrinkled,
Like ripples and waves
Of water
That fade before the kiss of shore,
Never knowing less,
Never wanting more.

Tears

If like tears,
my love for you,
would rain a thousand days.
Rivers swell to overflow
and drown the loveless ways.

If like wind,
my love for you,
would howl like hurricanes.
Ocean's spray on solid rock,
bathing coastal plains.

If like fire,
my love for you,
would flame a million years.
Enchanted star to seal a wish
and drive away the fear.

But, my love is human,
this I cannot measure.
All I have, I give to you,
a poor man's earthy treasure.

ocks

We are the rock-diggers.
Earth moving,
Stone cutting,
Big wheeled diesel,
Ground quaking,
Sky shaking
Road making,
Builders/boys
With hydraulic toys.

We are
Electric arc,
Detonation's spark,
Shattering ledge
Under tire tarps.

Others
Like/before us,
Painted caverns,
Chapels,
Erected pyramids,
Temples,
Created coliseums
And roads.

Our children
Will change
Horizons range,
Until
Dust we are no more.
Slumber's silent salute
To job well done.
Soft breezes on distant shore.

hunderstruck

Rain drops
Waterfall
Black sky,
Cloud wall.
We stand on fields
Of muck and gore,
Watching towers of ancient lore.

Clap hands,
Dance round,
Thunderclaps
Shake ground.
Lightening flashes…
Fingers
Long, hot, white,
As rain rides
Like wind swept pain.

Wet to the bone,
We run for cover,
Filled with freedom
Like newfound lover,
Each flash closer than the other,
No one remembers
The name of their mother.
Winds howl like
Hell's own furies,
As we, the peasants, tell our stories,
Take comfort
In memories,
Speak of fear not felt,
Heartbeats unheard,
Moments that pass
To silence at last…

oices

I hear voices,
Voices like minor chords,
Spanked on electric bass,
Sounds that run through the dark,
Branding the heart,
Heavy with the aromas
Of spices and spaces,
Like a smile among a million faces.
Tears meet
Over
Teacups politely filled
With secrets of dreams
That lay awake
Beside your head,
Filling your pillow with
Silent screams that echo
Echo
Like drums beating war
Whispering in rhythms
of death.
Telling tales,
Taking sales on
Stillness in the park,
Morning holds its' breath
Trying not to wake the homeless
Beneath the headlines
Holding down the park bench.

_W_alk

Some walk
So con-fi-dent,
Long stride,
Big pride,
Every move so
Im-por-tant.

Some take
Shorter
Hurried steps,
Hustling
To be here,
Or there,
Or just nowhere.

Some march
With slow
Deliberate
Gait.
Relying on
Earth to
Rotate
Beneath their feet.

Some stumble
And
Stagger
Fighting gravity's laws,
With padded paws
Shuffling the deck of time.

See upright ape,
Treetop dancer,
Like ballerina
Tiptoe dancer.
How large the shoe,
That wears the clown?

Driving

Speak:
Into empty
Windshield
filled with passing scenes,
pressed like flowers/dried
Between
Narrow
Headlight beams.

Words:
sound
so rich and round,
only to be found
Echoing
Hollow
Without truth
leaning near
with
understanding ear,
catching whispers
feeling through the fear.

Soul:
Like snowflakes
Fresh fallen,
Colored dark night blue
With red/rust/gold
Reflections of summer past
Wishing youth would last,
Until....
Dull
Humming
Wheel on road
Marks
Silence
on heavy load.
Quilted quiet
driving mode.

When...

Your desires
Burn
Like white hot
Phosphorous
Fires,
When
Thirst cries out
Of Dry/bone throat,
Think of me.
Cool quenching current
Of soothing comfortable love,
Flowing around
The next
Corner of river time,
Always seeking you-
The great mother earth
Like tributaries to the flood.
Be my inspiration,
I shall create,
Be my empress,
And I am your nation.
Be my love,
And I am yours.

Wind

I
Am
Wind.
Free to go
To be:
Scented kiss
On cheek and brow,
The hereafter
Of the here and now.
To be:
Cool breeze
After summer's day,
Or
Warm afternoon
At autumn's eve.
I take leaves.
Loose
My
Way
On forgotten trails.
I make:
The kite
Fly,
The trees talk,
Lovers listen as they walk,
Whisper,
Passing their fragrance to me
That I may trade with the flowers,
For pollen or pleasure,
Passing time,
I do not measure,
Spending moments
Like pirate treasure.
I am Wind.

Just a Moment

Once,
I killed the mastodon
To make your wedding ring.

Once,
I stole the emperor's canary,
So you could hear him sing.

Once a simple Knave,
Stole a kiss and more,
While his lordship
Fought and died,
On a heathen shore.

Once you spied
As a southern belle,
While I died
In Yankee hell.

Once,
I thought we had it right,
The flyer and the nurse,
Then bombs, rockets and exploding night,
Only made it worse.

Now here we are,
So very near,
Virgin hearts without fear.
I fall into your arms,
as the night whispers on,
Knowing nothing-
Nothing
Nothing at all.

Without

I am nothing,
but the dust of which I am made.
Yet, without you,
I, am less than that.

I am north wind
pasing through
bird filled branched,
yet without you,
I carry no song.

I am river
rolling wide
through green countryside,
yet without you,
I am endless desert sand.

I am star
winking across
a trillion galaxies,
yet, without you,
I am as darkest night.

I am fire
dancing
with a thousand sparks,
yet, without you,
I have no warmth.

I am dust,
or even less,
yet, without you,
I, am nothng at all.

you

With you, I am all things,
with your love, made whole.

With you, there is always
symphony playing love

With you, there is always
spring in heart and step.

With you, I am master of the
heavens, paled to your beauty.

With you, I burn with passion
hotter than the sun.

With you, I can do all.
with your faith, I love.

ighthouse

I call to her,
She beckons to me,
Lonely lighthouse-
Lovely sea.

Frothy foam of tongue and lip,
Lick the silent land,
Like footprints of a thousand paths
Form waves upon the sand.

Cargoes and carnage of empty emotions
Shipwreck on an unmarked reef.
All the joys of love
Mix freely with the waves of grief.

Like ghostly grenadiers at charge,
Surf falls short upon the shore-
Begging, pleading, needing,
Only to retreat once more.

The quiet lighthouse stands,
Thirsting eye on eternal sea.
I beckon to her,
She calls to me.

Wannabe

What do you wannabe,
When you're all grown up?
What will make you smile?
What makes it all worthwhile?

I wannabe a cowboy,
A playboy,
A professional sport,
A rich man, a wise man,
A likeable sort.

I wannabe an actor,
An activist,
An architect,
A bake, a builder,
Fly a jet!

I wannabe all
I've never been.
I want it all
To do over again.
What I've not done,
I'll never do,
I'll never have loved,
If I don't love you.

Out of the rain

One penny! Two penny!
Coppers down the drain,
Come in, my friend,
And get out of the rain.

It's warm inside,
Sit by the fire,
Have a plate,
Have a drink,
Whatever you desire.

One penny! Two penny!
Coppers down the drain.
Dark night, bad night,
To be out in the rain.

Laugh a little,
Drink a little,
Sit a little near,
Tell me stories, Tell me lies,
Just whisper in my ear.

One penny, two penny
Coppers down the drain.
Time keeps slipping, Dripping,
Out in the rain.

Now the grog
Weights your eyes,
As numbness fills your dreams.
I slash your purse, But not your throat,
Empty to the seams.

One penny! Two penny!
Coppers down the drain.
Come one, Come all,
Out of the rain.

about the author

STEPHEN P. REDIC

orn in Concord, New Hampshire and raised in Caribou, Maine, Stephen Redic is a true New Englander. A devout fan of the Red Sox, Patriots, and most importantly the Celtics, Stephen considers himself lucky to be supported by his equally devout wife, Pat. His experience with people, after 30 years in the retail industry, has provided a varied backdrop for what he writes about today. Preferring rural life, Stephen, Pat, and Bubba the Cat, now reside in Candia, New Hampshire in a house surrounded by trees and the sound of the winds.